Questioning Reality: Volume 1

Bobby Simonds

ISBN: **9781796407945**

ISBN 13: **XXXXX**

Library of Congress Control Number: **XXXXX**

LCCN Imprint Name: **City and State**

Front Cover & Editing by author.

bobby.simonds@gmail.com

www.facebook.com/bobbyraysimonds

www.facebook.com/bobbyrsimonds

www.instagram.com/@bobbysimonds

#bobbyraysimonds

#bobbysimonds

#BOBBYRAYSIMONDS

#ATWISTINTRAVEL

#risenfromtheashes

#toxicamerica

#Challenge-thyself

#avoidinghavoc

#QUESTIONINGREALITY

Chapter 1

There have been many people over the thousands – and even millions – of generations that humans have been attempting to strive to the top. Like so many, I myself, have striving to get thru the rankings of other various top authors. But in a digital age, it's easier to publish, but more difficult to be noticed.

In any field of accomplishments, there will always be challenges that you never would seem to predict. In my field, it's marketing. Without a good strategy of marketing, I will never truly be recognized for my hard work, and years of dedication.

I strongly feel that I have the potential to be known as one of the greatest authors of not just my own time (generation); but in others to come. This doesn't come from ego, or arrogance. This comes from a feeling that I've had since childhood. The only issue is, that there seems to be a "higher" power that is keeping me from doing so. Whether it's the *Universe* that is constantly testing my abilities, and even my level of patience.

I have accomplished much since my first book was published nearly 5 years ago. What seems like yesterday, isn't. I have published over 50 books. Many of which are short, and long, non-fiction books. Of course, I have a 4-part series, *A Twist in Travel*; a single novel, *Avoiding*

Havoc; a starter series (not sure if I will continue at this point in time), *Hell Has Risen.* In addition to my fictional pieces, I am stuck on a really good thriller/suspense novel. Nonetheless, I have had my share of failures too. One of which, is learning the hardest way with the writing-competitions. I have learned that they are all rigged. They aren't looking for new talent. They're looking for well-established authors that have a) graduated from college; or b) are already published [and/or] have been currently/previously published by smaller companies (not amazon.com). That said, if you do a google search for top sellers, that will also put me out to the curb. However, if you do the same search with my name (as the main search – *Bobby*

Simonds), I will be on the first few pages

supported for your search. But how in the hell do

I get my name down as a faster search? Hitting

the top charts, or paying to get there!

Chapter 2

Have you ever had one of those days that throws your mind-setting out to the *bleachers*? I have. More than I can count. Sometimes it may be a thought that I had, a sight that my mind attempted to explain away, or just a theory that comes to mind.

More often than not, I believe that we've all had *one of those days*. This book isn't a comparison to others; moreover, it's about the many experiences, and/or thoughts that have popped in my mind, that I just couldn't shake, that threw me off for the entire day. If you're nodding your head while reading this, then stay tuned, because this book is certainly for you!

If you had read any of my past books, then you would know that I am not keen on religion. I understand its purpose, the right to believe, and the right for those who would like to be sheep. I feel the exact same way with politics, and much of how our entire world/reality is even structured, in a sense what seems to be for those with an emotional misperception.

With my opinions [and theories], I have come to realize that I am here to express to those who may be on the edge of understanding. My purpose is to give that extra nudge, for those who are curious what authors may be considering to be fact. Rather than fiction. I have written well over twenty books on these related topics. Therefore, this series isn't a stretch, in comparison with my other series'. Such series include (newest to oldest):

    *Toxic America

    *Risen from the Ashes

    *The True Masterminds of Manipulation

    *first nonfiction series

That said, **one of those days** only seems fitting to create. As I have often had many of those confusing days, that throws my mind into a whirlwind!

I often keep an eye on *reviews* that "readers" leave. There have been a few that I have "red-flagged" because there are those of "power/influence" attempting to sway anyone from reading some of my books. Which I send messages to these people, and never once have they responded to their *hateful* reviews. In fact, I rarely get reviews, but I do sell quite a few books each month since April of 2014. It's hard to believe that I've been doing this for nearly five years!

In any regard, with the 3-4 bogus reviews, I've only had about a dozen [or less] that <u>real</u> people have even commented on books read, from my list.

I have come across many other authors that are running into this problem, so it's not just me; although at the time, I had thought it was!

The hate that people write about towards books, that they deemed un-fit to read, or be seen by others, is quite shocking. You wouldn't think that there would be a set-crowd that goes about writing bogus, yet snotty, reviews from books they've never purchased. Why even take the time to do so? If you wonder why – as I had once did – I'll let you in on a little secret: I'm doing something right. Because the only time people around me, seem to hate on my books, are envious, and they wish I wasn't that intelligent! What else would explain such stupidity?

As an author, I find the last year to be slow. In 2017 I had published 18 various titles. In 2018, less than a dozen. I had a busy year, but I am excited about 2019. Why, you may ask?

Because I plan on hitting 20! I have high hopes for myself. With this series, and a few miscellaneous fiction stories that I am working on, I'm certain that this year will be great. My goal by next January (2020), is to have 75 available titles. Which means, I have to get my ass in gear, and step on my *Creative Gas-Pedal!*

Next month, I will be joining the *online college community*. I believe that I am finally ready. I figured I will be nearly 50, by the time I graduate, along with my wife.

Chapter 3

Getting on with the story. I apologize for rambling! I cannot help myself to talk to you, as you are sitting across from me. Which, I would be rambling then too!

I have come to realize that with all the jobs I have held down, I still best serve myself, and the public best, with my writing. I spent majority of 2018 working outside of my house. It's difficult not to, since my books haven't brought in much money yet. Even in this day in age, we still need traditional publishers to help support creative, long-lasting authors. All the same, I want to thank you in advance for your support!

Today I was driving home from grocery shopping. The air: crisp. The sky, filled with scattered clouds, with the sun pushing its gleaming powers through my windshield: blinding me!

During this temporary blindness (before my eyes became blurry), I noticed something between the sun and the clouds. It sounds nuts, but I swear I saw an island, within this space in the sky. It was hazy, but I am certain as to what I saw. It was almost iridescent, but as clear as day, I could make out the island's edge, grass to the edge, followed with dirt at the cliff's edge, leading downward. It was strange, yet fast. For once, my mind didn't attempt to explain it away. Because it knew exactly what it had just seen. It thru my mind off, but I continued with my drive, and put

it in the back of my mind, and put it into this

book!

Chapter 4

You ever have one of those days… It's your second week on the job, you're somewhat excited, because it's new, it's different…

Then you arrive at work, and you're ready to finish up your training. But guess what? Pop quiz…it's open-notes, and you're stoked because your notes are perfect. Then you take the test. It's gotta be a passing percentage, your job is on the line. You think to yourself, *I've got this, no problem*!

Soon after you take the 50-part-question quiz, you await the test results. To your surprise, you fail the test, because of missing two-extra questions, that worded so wrong, that even your perfect notes couldn't support the answers for you.

Soon after, you find out that you must have an 85% to pass. You failed it with an 80%. Then your instructor informs you to retake, warning you that the questions will be worded differently.

You take a swift break, to clear your mind from whatever questions you may have misguided yourself into choosing the wrong answers.

You seat yourself back down, in front of that computer that you would love nothing more to chuck thru the nearby window!

Then, you retake the same test – worded quite differently. You become confused halfway in, because you come to realize that the exam is

rigged somehow. Because after you finish, you

now receive a 60%. Um…yeah that just

happened! You get up, beyond enraged. You

finish up your work-day.

After work, you get home, stressed because

you know the truth about what happens the

following morning when you are meant to work.

A long restless night follows, leaving you in

despair of only one-hours' sleep. The drive is

grueling, longer than usual. The twenty-two-

minute drive seems to take like an hour instead;

because you are dreading of what you already are

aware of what is about to happen to you.

At last, you arrive to work. You no longer enter the building to be told to go to the conference room. You didn't even bring in anything of importance, knowing your job is done.

Your boss points to the chair from across him/her. Then, while you try to control your breathing, you see your bosses' lips moving, the only thing you hear is: *Sorry we have to let you go, you failed the exam, that you had taken twice.*

A bunch of words follow, but you're too focused inside your mind, being murdered by your own thoughts. Then you shake the persons hand, exit the building. Sit in your car for a moment, before peeling out of the parking lot, and get home in a matter of minutes from driving

too damn fast!

Yeah, you ever have one of those days?

Chapter 5

The day finally arrives when you are on the look-out for every cop that is working the streets. Your tags expired, and your muffler is louder than a Harley on steroids!

The giant hole in the muffler is more like a crater; the pipe has rotted out, and bottomed out weeks ago. The end of the year has arrived, and everything should have been mechanically fixed months ago. To add to your torment, you're six thousand miles overdue on your oil change from a job that terminated you for failing an exam.

Not two-minutes away from your home, reality sets in, and the "pretty" flashing lights on top of that pesky police cruiser, pulls up behind you.

You somehow manage to get a verbal for your tags, but then get butt-fucked from your muffler!

One week to the day, your wife gets a ticket for her expired tags. *Two wrongs, don't make a right.* Was the first thought in my mind!

Chapter 6

A cold winters' day, is a quiet one. For
some reason, or another, during winter, the air
becomes so silent, that it becomes eerie. The only
sounds that can be heard, is the passing motorists,
a train from a few miles from home, and the
occasional wild bird squawking. Of course, you
can hear a dog bark, too. Especially, mine!

Nevertheless, when it's that silent – day or
night – you know when something isn't right,
when random noises occur.

Last week, for example, sounded as though
a woman were screaming. The scream that you
never forget, when you've heard it when you
were younger. The sound of pain, close to death,

from something bad happening. But the location

where your ears direct you are in two different

directions. Both of which, would be impossible

for a human's pinpoint. In one direction, water: a

marsh. The second, above your…house?

Chapter **7**

Have you noticed lately with how many human beings are no longer looking up? It reminds me of when I walk my dog. Their snout is too busy aiming at the ground. Just like with humans, for the past few years. These smart phones are making us (humans) dumber than shit. We no longer look up, unless it's a big enough distraction to pull us away from our phones. All the pretty pictures, colors, and games…Oh, my!

It makes me wonder, more often than it should, why these devices are even allowed. Between the future health risks, the risk of present & future dumbness it's creating for the majority - like we need help, to make us dumber! Not to mention, if we're all looking down, how would we know what's lingering in the sky, or streaking

across the sky? Nobody ever looks up anymore.

Doesn't this make anybody question why we're

being manipulated by our phones to look down,

rather than keep an eye on what may be right

above us?

It makes me wonder, mainly after the 1997

Arizona Lights, and the other mass sightings with

UFOs. With all the rumors online, and on

television shows, along with plenty of books

being written (myself included); it makes the

creators of these things wonder what may be

coming. Or is "it" already here, or about to be?

It may not be alien. It may come to war on

our own soil. Is that partly the reason why

President Trump removed so many troops

overseas?

It could be due to the preparation for the

Mexico/American wall being built. It could be

aliens. War. Some invasion, which none of us

will see coming, before it's too late, because the

100% of cell phone users are too busy looking

down!

Chapter 8

My biggest question for humanity is, *why are creative people so different than the rest of the 'heard'?* Is it because the 1-2% that are creative, are designed this way from the moment our mothers were impregnated by our fathers? Were our spirits taught this before being sent to our mothers' womb? Furthermore, during these "teachings", why are some of us (the creative types), threaded for such an art of creation, that some of us sing, write, paint, and build such magnificence, when others only believe that they have the abilities to do the same, when they clearly don't. Which when majority of these "failures" realize it to be to late, that they're made a mockery of. Whether it's from an appearance on a television show, or from their inner circles…

The ability that is given to create comes a huge responsibility. We become teachers, heroes, legends, masterminds, entertainers, brothers, sisters, spiritual healers, and so on. The people that make it in society stick out like a soar thumb. The ones that know they have what it takes (like many, like myself), are put thru obstacles, life challenges and/or failures, that we have to struggle with every thought, every moment, every set-back, that we question everything in our paths.

Our paths change constantly. We hurdle, we lunge, we progress. Some fail, due to the longest struggles that seem like they're stuck within an inner hell. We all have a hell, but for the creative souls like myself, feel as though, that we may never progressing past the level that we're currently in, that majority either give up entirely, or commit suicide, because they cannot foresee their futures.

I suppose the purpose for this, is that those failures, those who give up easily, really aren't ready to proceed with a "new" way of life. The life that all humans want. The life with more "freedoms" due to a financial gain, that they currently don't have, while striving for what they believe that they have the right to have.

What many of those types of people have in common that give up what they feel [and believe] that should be theirs, is that they aren't great with handling people.

Just imagine this:

*Somebody that has the worst self-confidence, and a bad self-image, around hundreds, and thousands (or hundreds of thousands) of new-found fans, rushing at them in public. How do you think somebody like that would react? Badly, very badly. They would end up committing suicide – like Kurt Cobain (perhaps). Or they would react violently towards another fan, despite that "person" being a fan. All because they weren't ready for what they had believed to be theirs, in the first place.

Many newly-found authors get their books put on the top sellers list. They continue writing, until their series comes to an end. Because this same series (fiction, of course) will end up being a blockbuster hit at the movies. The gain a ton of money, but don't see the bigger picture. They don't realize that with all the hard work they've accomplished, that it doesn't (and shouldn't) stop with that.

Stephenie Meyer wrote one the best series of all time: Twilight. It was one of the most compelling, yet accomplished series that had gone from best-seller, to best blockbuster. She literally wrote only a few other books; that had nothing to do with what has been phrased as, *The Twilight saga.*

Then there's **J.K. Rowling**. She is known for **Harry Potter** of course, and her book series has sold over 500 million. Just think if that series had been given up on, by either the publisher or agent.

What if the author herself, had given up half way thru the series, because it was all about the money that she had achieved during her success?

There are many one-hit wonders, that didn't push thru the chaos that came with being in the spotlight. None of which, that I will delve into. Nevertheless, when it comes to music, there are more than a few hundred that made it in the industry, that had become known as that ***1-hit-wonder***. Because they wanted to have fame for a minute, not a life-long adventure.

I do believe that those 1-hit-wonders are no different in the writing business. Only now-a-days, we're stuck with Amazon.com. We have to buy our way thru to get to the top of the best-selling list, before people start purchasing our books for the masses. A lot of this is marketing, not word of mouth. Not chance. Unless of course, you get traditionally published, and that publisher does all the marketing for you. Again, they don't teach you how to deal with fame, or success. This is something you must learn on your own time. Nevertheless, majority of the greats (for authors), are generally college educated. Even though, majority of these same writers already had what it took, but they needed a college education to get noticed.

J.K. Rowling, Stephen King, Tom Robins, T.S. Eliot, and Judy Blume were college grads (and many more of course). These were just to name a few.

To list a few legendary authors/writers that

didn't attend college:

- Ray Bradbury
- Maya Angelou
- Truman Capote
- Mark Twain
- H. G. Wells
- Jack London
- Augusten Burroughs
- Charles Dickens
    …and more.

Chapter 9

What makes us, us?

Is it our experiences? Which ones do you think? Because we have many experiences that could make us who we are today, and even in the future.

I remember back when I was a kid, just beginning school. I had a gym teacher that did things to me after school, for two years. Then I thought I was fortunate by switching elementary schools (from 1st to 2nd grade). I was so happy, and relieved, until I had begun the next school.

Since being born with Mild Cerebral Palsy; I was forced to wear a back-brace. The purpose for it was to help my muscles in my back develop properly. Whether it helped or not, I cannot tell you. That really isn't my point.

Nevertheless, I had to go to school to wear this damn thing, and the school nurse was supposed to check it everyday to examine me; mainly to make sure it was doing "its" job.

Mind you, this was just the school nurse. Not long after, there were more people. Four regular teachers, the nurse, the assistant principal, and the principle. All these assholes had "inspected" me…from 2nd grade until the middle of 4th grade. I became an angry little child on the "playing-field" to say the least. I wasn't a bully. I was a protector. I managed to bully my way into this spot, but I then became a protector for the other kids. Younger or older, I watched over them, to keep the bullies out, and stop the

nonsense of being picked on, laughed at (because

of abnormalities), and even stop kids from getting

their lunch money stolen. And no, I didn't take

their money either.

I even had a friend that I was told that he

had fingered a girl (a girlfriend of mine at the

time, I had many in school), that was obviously

without her consent. I didn't believe that he

could do such a thing, and didn't believe the girl

at the time. Not long after she expressed to me

with what had happened, I had other friends tell

me about the circumstance, because this kid was

bragging about how he not only was able to do

this act, but get away with it – so he thought.

I decided to confront this kid after school. He admitted it, assuming I wasn't going to do anything about it, because he was a "purple-belt". That didn't stop me, because I clocked him, off-guard; and broke his nose, and his eye-glasses. Needless to say, his mother tried pressing charges on me, and the school. Then the police learned quickly that he sexually assaulted another girl, and the charges were placed on him.

When the drama of the sexual abuse had stopped that I had received, I learned – along with my parents – that telling the truth, doesn't always work in your favor. The teachers and nurse were suspended without pay during the "investigation." Then, once the board came to a ruling, nothing was done. My parents decided to put the house up for sale, and move to California to where my mothers' parents had moved a couple of years before. It was the best thing that happened to me – for the most part.

Looking back on these grotesque acts from two different schools in New York, I wonder if this made me so stubborn, less communicative, and eager to help others, aside from myself. I wonder if the reason why I'd like to become a Family Counselor (a dream of mine since 2015), has something to do with my own experience that I had unfortunately received as a child, or a writer for that matter.

I often wonder how I became an author/writer. What experience had brought on me writing non-fiction, verses fiction. And why I write various books for non-fiction to begin with.

It seems like I have more questions than answers,

but it does make me look more closely at my life,

as to why I am the way I am.

Chapter 10

As many of you already may be aware; I do

majority of my research on Youtube.com. It is

about the only place where you can get your

option with just about any subject, as far as,

documentaries go.

That said, I recently had watched a doc

about how the Navy has been back-engineering

from Extra-Terrestrials saucers. Moreover, not

only have they been doing this since the mid to

late 1940s, but they've been successful with

doing so.

According to the many retiree's, we have

been in deep-space exploration since the late

1960s. They also express that we didn't officially

land on the moon – as I had once theorized. The

original moon-landing footage from what millions

of people all around the globe had seen, was in

fact, created at Area 51 (and from Hollywood).

If anyone doubts this, all you need to do, is

watch the footage and listen. Watch the flag – it

moves. There is no wind in space. There isn't

any engine noise upon landing onto the moon.

You cannot hear the "thrusters" from the bottom

of the craft, upon landing. This isn't possible,

when you can hear the voices. Furthermore,

where the fuck are the stars? The background is

pitch-black. All we have to do is be observant.

Only the idiot's in this world believes this

garbage. They are easily manipulated!

My book, Toxic America: The Dome Effect, published September 1, 2018; was absolutely correct too. We live in a dome. It's obvious to me, and many others that are labeled as crazy, nut-jobs, or even conspiracy theorists – in today's society, when speaking of the obvious possibility.

In any case, if you look back to when they continued launching the old-fashioned rocket ships, they exploded over and over. I believe that the reason for that, was because they continued hitting the top of the "globe".

If you pay attention to past & present President speeches, they've all admitted from time to time, that we live in a dome, and that we have never landed on the moon.

The issue isn't leaving Earth's atmosphere, it's camouflaging it.

We cannot simply go up, but we must go thru portals. These various (and many) portals get us off this planet, and into space, along with localized planets (and even the moon).

Many Ufologists had always theorized this notion, but could never prove their theories. Mainly because, if you think Area 51 was is heavily guarded, just imagine the areas with the portals!

Another thing that many of these retiree's discuss – aside from space travel; is that we have been living amongst alien entities since the beginning. We're not speaking of the Grey's, or the *tall whites*, we're speaking of extra-

terrestrial's that look almost identical as humans –

yeah, that's right.

That can't be true, it's too science fiction!

Chapter 11

`Since Hollywood has begun, it seems that our government has been using storytellers to bring to film, the concept of aliens. They give us storylines with both harmful, and welcoming aliens alike. In the movie, *Battle of Los Angeles*, this was more or less, a fictional documentary. If you look into it, it actually took place. Weird right?

War of the worlds was a story that was first heard on a radio show, to test how humanity would handle an alien-invasion, if it had taken place. As they – I'm certain – predicted, the public [at the time] had failed. Therefore, they kept us out of the loop.

I often wonder if we had acted rationally, with hearing the initial broadcast, if "they" would have kept us in the loop, and put all these buried secrets into the open, including textbooks in our school system.

One day, they will openly discuss aliens, as though it were always an open-discussion. One day, we will be learning of these extra-terrestrials in our schools – for generations to come. And, one day, we will act rationally about an invasion – if it came down to it – because we will be taught about the various races. One day…

With all that said, it makes me also wonder, why people always assume that we're at war with another country, knowing we [as American's] having nothing to gain. Such as Vietnam.

If you take a look at all the wars America was involved with (except for WWI & WWII), there seemed to have always been a hidden agenda with America. Whether it was a take-over, or oil. There was always a bigger picture, that the civilians in my country hadn't considered. The media was used in such a way, that nobody would have guessed otherwise. 9/11 was obviously a set-up, based on the way it was orchestrated. That was literally the only time, our acting President had ignored the situation. Therefore, he knew about it prior; and was most likely told not to intervene, by the "higher-ups."

Chapter 12

Questioning reality is everything. This isn't conspiracy. It's human.

My friends & family often think that my theories are too far-fetched. Nonetheless, there seems to be a circle for people like me – and I don't talk in that circle. I listen. I observe. It's important to take yourself out of the level of "craziness" that people label us. Nevertheless, the reality that we were born in, has a ton of hidden realities, mixing into ours.

Aliens, and/or, extra-terrestrials, are obviously real. There are many races, like humans. The live among us, and travel above us. They meet with our governments, and military commanders, and even our scientists, and engineers. But *we as the people* have been misled for centuries. There has been a hidden agenda, it could be greed, it could be power, it could be fear, even. What ever the reason, *we as the people* should be sticking together. Not for the sake of humanity, but more or less, the *greater good.*

Just consider how the police disregard neighborhoods that have a high criminal rate. How often in these same areas that the police don't even come to help these families?

Now, consider the same scenario, only with alien's coming to earth – in a bad way. You think our government will be there for you?

Chapter 13

I was watching another video on Youtube.com the other day. It was showing how a rocket that was meant to go into space, blew up. It also showed how the rocket didn't go straight up, as we are meant to perceive. It also showed the rocket exploding, just before it was supposed to leave our atmosphere, into space.

After reviewing the footage a few times, I conclude that we do live in a dome. The evidence is clear to me, as to the other 1% dome-believers. It doesn't necessarily mean we're nuts. Moreover, it means we're believing our guts, our minds, and our brains.

I also was watching a show the other day, not sure the name (fell asleep shortly after). They mentioned in the show, that the creative-types in this world use their left brains; while the "normal" folks use their right. I never realized that, nor, did I ever consider it. It makes perfect sense.

Chapter 14

What is it about pain, that many of us feel that we must have a supplement in place? It begins as a simple, and quick bandage. Then it becomes a permanent replacement, for a tolerance we never seemed to carry.

From what many of us know, that aren't taking pills, as supplement… We know the dangers of the excessive usage from these "permanent-bandages." I know for first-hand, from watching my mother take them. Her mind is in a constant denial of many things; negativity is in complete control. Very little ambition, bitchiness, forgetfulness – like you wouldn't believe. These are just some examples from what I've witnessed in just five years.

Doctors love people like my mother. Those of you who are frequent fliers at the doctors, will get pissed; nonetheless, doctors are, in my opinion, educated bullshitters. They obviously learn a great deal of symptoms. Regardless, as far as treatment is concerned, they don't give a rat's ass about healing us. They are in it for the money, just like the FDA (Federal Drug Administration).

Speaking of the FDA, how many times has somebody come up with a cure for cancer, aides, polio, and other gnarly, devastating/deadly diseases? How many of these has been approved by the FDA, and had been brought to our attention in a "vaccine" form? We're all idiots, we take, we accept, we don't get better…Yet, we don't point the finger at the vaccine, we point the

finger at a new symptom. And that's the trick,

that they've succeeded, with.

For years, we've been told it's best,

recommended to take advantage of any vaccines

provided by our government. Majority of us, take

advantage. Assuming we won't get, whatever

disease it's meant to fight. Such as, the flu virus.

I can't speak for everyone, but in the past, when I

did so, I ended up with the whooping cough,

bronchitis, and the flu strain. Accordingly, what

was the point? I stopped taking the vaccines, and

I only get sick 2-3 times per year. And I'm a

smoker!

Often, I suffer from mild, to severe,

migraine headaches. Therefore, I wait until its

get's past the point, I can barely function –

mobilization, concentration, dizziness – and then

I am forced to take something for it. I've only

had one thing that has worked (since I was 15,

when I first began getting them). Naproxen.

Ironically, it's not meant for migraines, yet it

works wonders – as long as you don't mind

feeling stupid for a day or two.

When I have **_Hydrocodone_** on hand, this

works wonders for energy, small pain, &

concentration. It's a wanna-be version on

Vicodin; yet the Vicodin never worked for me – if

anything, it made me nauseous. As far as,

Hydrocodone, is concerned, the .750

milligrams worked best. Anything higher, feels

as though you were, hypothetically speaking, *hit*

by a freight train!

Chapter 15

I have covered what I am about to share in several other books I had written. I find it to be trivial to this book, with *Questioning Reality*.

As far as those who experience being unemployed, such as myself, I find it strange how difficult it is to find work. There are many jobs to be found online. Whether it'd be retail, restaurant, fast-food, dirty jobs, maintenance, to real careers; there doesn't seem to be a shortage. Yet, every time I find myself unemployed, I can't just pick up a job the next day, let alone three months later. Therefore, what the fuck?

Is it part of the cosmic plan, to get to rock bottom, before you are allowed the opportunity for your next position – whatever that may be?

I also find it ironic for those who "make it" in the entertainment business, that they too (majority of them, that is) have all went from job-to-job. Of course, there are those (lucky ones), who never had an issue keeping employment.

I went from keeping a job, and a happy marriage (as far as, the financial support of marriage), to hitting rock bottom. I landed a job within two months, but was let go, due to not passing a test for training (which I for one, thought was rigged). In addition, that was back in December of 2018. Currently, we're going into the middle of February of 2019 (just after the government was "turned back on"); three interviews, that led nowhere; and about 200-250 applications. No call backs, no follow-up emails. It's as though I've entered a dark alley. Furthermore, bills are stacking, and the marriage is on the line, yet again.

So, who is controlling me? Why aren't the "higher-ups" or my "avatar" allowing me to get a job? You may be wondering why I don't "pray" to "Jesus" or "God." Nonetheless, how much has religion truly assisted you? Earth clearly isn't about happiness, since drama seems to be on all the headlines. God wants "his" children to experience happiness, and equality. Withal, I have only experienced glimpses if any. People may also wonder why I don't just change my attitude. Or simply attempt to attract the job I may desire. Let me tell you, I have, and that too has gotten me nowhere.

Reality is a fucked-up illusion that we must truly learn to associate with. It's not about survival. It's not about pride, power, love, or anything else. It becomes more and more clear to me, that we live in a simulation, based on my experiences, and others that share my theories.

Nonetheless, this shit has to stop. Why is it that the good people always seem to get fucked in the end? Should I become a criminal, join politics? I am currently in the process of joining the "higher education population." However, I still have to pay bills, and I can't even land a job at McDonald's!

From dealing with my constant mental theories, and dealing with what's right in front of me, I now fully understand why my father checked out, when he did. Life sure as hell isn't easy. But when you always try to do right, and stay on the "straight & narrow", it seems like complete bullshit when you find yourself at the bottom, of the largest pit in life. Failure isn't the issue, because I'm successful with my books (not at the top, not by a long shot). But I am an international author, with over 50, plus books. That's a ton, considering my first book was published April of 2014!

I do like to brag about that, since I didn't attend college for "English/Creative Writing." Those that don't have the passion, but yearn for it; assuming that college will train you to become the next big author – yet majority of the big-shots, didn't need college; but it doesn't hurt to better craft your style, and/or stories.

Being told from your family, and even your spouse – almost on the daily [which feels hourly at times] – can be quite difficult, when attempting to gain employment is out of your control. They lecture you with threats, assuming that the reason why you haven't found employment, is your own demise. It isn't, I for one, can tell you that.

Many jobs that I had applied to [those of which, had contacted me], claim that these various positions are "entry-level", yet, when they go over your experience, you don't qualify.

Hmm… It sounds like an underlying, double-

standard, if you ask me.

Chapter 16

It's astonishing to listen to my parents' generations, when they discuss the moon landing, that they had "witnessed" on television. Along with hearing the news of the Kennedy Assassination. I'm surprised that our government didn't lie even more than they already had back in the sixties!

Not to place blame, or point fingers here, but those of you who lived in the sixties were so damn gullible. How in the fuck did you believe that the moon landing was ever real? Let alone that *Lee Harvey Oswald* killed Kennedy when he wasn't even at the place of murder? I'm so glad that I was born in 1980, I would have been labeled a communist!

I suppose "they" being the citizens of America, would easily be swayed, seeming how the internet wasn't brought to the public. I could understand assuming that your government would never lie to us, would be easily persuaded. Especially, when our President was murdered. It still surprises me, however, that our country hasn't rioted when reporters dug deep enough, in the 2000's, to prove that Lee Harvey Oswald wasn't the shooter; and that, the FBI & CIA were behind the murder. It really shocks me, that our own agencies can get away with murder, so easily, if orchestrated properly.

The same can be said for the moon landing, of course. But I won't go there again!

What I will bring up, however, is the fake food supplements, which are forcing farmers to close shop. And those farmers that refuse, all of a sudden are dealing with floods, that destroy their crops. Ironic isn't it?

We have a fake food ingredient for just about anything now. Especially, with sugar. They say, that an ingredient – which is approved by the FDA – can kill a person over time. It's called: *bromine.*

To better equip your brain around this one, here's a link that has a story on the top 9 foods that carry toxins:

https://www.shape.com/healthy-eating/diet-tips/9-common-foods-contain-toxic-ingredients

Chapter 17

Donald Trump's mission as a President was building a 2,000-mile wall to separate America from Mexico. But why? And why did he "shut-down-the-government" to accomplish this in late 2018, to early 2019? Here's my theory:

*I highly doubt it's to keep drugs out, because there's always the ports of the coast, digging tunnels under the wall, after it's built, and crossing the line from Canada. It's not to keep immigrant's out, because we all know that America was built from immigration. In my highest opinion, I strongly believe that it will keep virus's out – such as the one created from China a few years back, that turned many humans into Science-fact, **Zombies!** I also believe, that it* *could be place for other purposes, such as real aliens. When we eventually go into a real war, that we aren't blinded with seeing, and whatever may not be flying in saucers, will crumble us on foot. There is a much bigger picture here, that isn't clear to any of us, but we can all speculate, obviously. Call me strange, call me crazy, but it sure isn't to keep Mexican's our, or American's in, that's for fucking sure!*

The *war on drugs* is no different than *the war on terrorism, & the war on guns.* Did you know, that majority of the money that funds the CIA, is actually drug money? And why the hell do we even label it as drug money, in the first place? I'm sure that money was hard worked for, and those individuals that used it to buy the drugs, even paid their taxes!

The *war on terrorism* is just another way to get the fear factor into check, and get more approval from the "public" to "allow" us to go to war. I bet you never knew that Obama Bin Laden once worked for the CIA, all the way up until his death in fact!

The war on guns, well it's simple. The government takes our weapons away, so when they initiate Martial Law, we don't have anything to defend ourselves, except for pitch-forks, and knifes.

The claims our media/government and other agencies (such as MK-ULTRA), have such a lock on our minds, that we never truly think twice about what the consequences will be after everything is said and done. We support those families who died from terrorism. We support those families who died from school shootings across America. We also support those families who die of drugs. But in the end, we support our lying-through-the-teeth government? Because the bigger picture here, ladies & gents, is to lose our freedom (which seems like we never really had), to lose our right to defend ourselves, and the right to take any stand against foreign and domestic soldiers. This is insane right? Those were just words written on a document named, *The Constitutional Rights* (a.k.a., the amendments).

As I mentioned before, I'm not crazy, I'm not a conspirator, when it's obvious to me, because I do my fair share of research. I also get these theories rattling around in my mind, until I write them down in my many books, to help better educate those around me. Therefore, you can't call me bluff, but perhaps you can call "theirs" (our 'leaders').

Thanks again for purchasing this book, and I look forward to reading your reviews. You can always send me a message on my FaceBook page (private chat preferred). You can also email me, as I am always checking it anyway. The following pages includes my book listings that you can purchase at most online retailers. Thanks again!

Books from Bobby Simonds:

1) A twist in travel: Fate (sci-fi)

2) The incident of 12/6/14 (nonfiction)

3) A twist in travel: Scientific Wastelands (sci-fi)

4) J.J.'s Rhymin' Adventures: The Complete Series (kid's poetry)

5) The True Masterminds of Manipulation: Volume 1 (nonfiction)

6) The True Masterminds of Manipulation: Volume 2 (nonfiction)

7) The True Masterminds of Manipulation: Volume 3 (nonfiction)

8) Living with Mild Cerebral Palsy (bio)

9) The true masterminds of manipulation: The complete series (nonfiction)

10) An angry memo: attention all humans (nonfiction)

11) Mind boggling experiences of the weird & strange (nonfiction/paranormal)

12) Missing my dog, my best friend: Ginger (nonfiction/self-help)

13) Don't mind the little things! (nonfiction/self-help)

14) Where are all the good drivers?

(nonfiction/self-help/educational)

15) Puggle fun with Ginger (picture book, young children)

16) Do you have what it takes to become the next great author? (nonfiction/self-help/guidance/educational)

17) Family in Ruins: The loss from a suicide (nonfiction/self-help/guidance)

18) What is banned in America: Volume 1 (nonfiction/awareness)

19) Risen from the Ashes: Untold Truths & Theories (Volume 1; Political Awareness/nonfiction)

20) Empty Conversations: Dear Dad (nonfiction/grievance)

21) Risen from the Ashes: You be the judge (volume 2; nonfiction/political awareness)

22) Risen from the Ashes: Surrounded by Stupid's (Volume 3; nonfiction/political awareness)

23) Risen from the Ashes: Living in an Unjust Society (Volume 4; nonfiction/political awareness)

24) A Twist in Travel: The End is Near (sci-fi/series)

25) Risen from the Ashes: Broken Shackles, Part 1 (Volume 5; nonfiction/political awareness)

26) Where are all the good drivers? Driving in Upstate New York (Volume 2; nonfiction/education/awareness)

27) Risen from the Ashes: Broken Shackles, Part 2 (Volume 6; nonfiction/political awareness)

28) Risen from the Ashes: Broken Shackles, Two-Fer (Volume 7; nonfiction/political awareness)

29) A Twist in Travel: The Final Journey (science fiction/action; volume 4; end of series)

30) Risen from the Ashes: Identity Crisis (nonfiction; volume 8)

31) Risen from the Ashes: The First 8 (nonfiction; volume 9)

32) Risen from the Ashes: Imprisoning America (nonfiction; volume 10, end)

33) Challenge thy-self: Phase 1 (nonfiction; philosophy, self-help; volume 1)

34) Challenge thy-self: Phase 2 (nonfiction; philosophy, self-help; volume 2)

35) Challenge thy-self: Phase 3 (nonfiction; philosophy, self-help; volume 3)

36) Challenge thy-self: The complete Set (nonfiction; philosophy, self-help; All three phases combined)

37) CNY: Customer Awareness (nonfiction; reviews)

38) Avoiding Havoc (single Novel, fiction; Suspense, Thriller, Action)

39) A Twist in Travel: The Complete Series (Sci-fi/Fantasy/Adventure/fiction/humor)

40) Toxic America: We Shall Obey! (Volume 1; nonfiction; self-awareness)

41) Toxic America: Concealing America (Volume 2; nonfiction; self-awareness)

42) Toxic America: The Conspiracy of They (Volume 3; nonfiction; self-awareness)

43) Bobby's Creative Photography Series: Volume 1 (nonfiction; photography)

44) Bobby's Creative Photography Series: Volume 2 (nonfiction; photography)

45) Bobby's Creative Photography Series: Volume 3 (nonfiction; photography)

46) Toxic America: The Perfect Simulation (Volume 4; nonfiction)

47) Toxic America: Broken Barriers (volume 5; nonfiction)

48) Toxic America: Crude Awakenings! (volume 6; nonfiction)

49) Toxic America: America's Emotional Distress (volume 7; nonfiction)

50) Toxic America: The Dome Effect (volume 8; nonfiction)

51) Hell has risen: Painstricken (volume 1;
fiction; dark fantasy/thriller; suspense)

52) Toxic America: The Complete Series
(Volumes 1-8; Nonfiction)

53) Questioning Reality: Volume 1(nonfiction;
self-help; conspiracy; political)

<u>**THANK YOU, DEAREST READER!**</u>

www.ingramcontent.com/pod-product-compliance
Lightning Source LLC
Chambersburg PA
CBHW070815240726
48654CB00007B/365